Creative Conflict Solving For Kids

Fran Schmidt and Alice Friedman

Illustrations by Teresa Solotoff
I-Care Cat Illustrations by Rebecca Poole-Heyne
Graphic Design by Ralph Schmidt
Cover Design by Chris Heyne

Acknowledgements

Special thanks to **:**

Elyse Brunt for her poems "Sometimes," "My Temperature's Rising," and "It's Not My Fault!"

Jean Marvel for her input on the mediation role plays.

Norma Minges and her gifted students at **Springview Elementary School** for the "Fighting Fair Flair."

Shirley Morton for her stories "The First Day," "Where Can He Be?", "The Bully."

Ellie Stein for her design ideas.

Shirley Zundel, Leah Jaffe, Elysse Brunt, and **Shirley Wuchter** for proofreading.

Hi Boys and Girls!

My name is I-Care-Cat and I am a peacemaker. I'm here to help you become a peacemaker and an I-Care-Kid.

This year you will have the wonderful opportunity to learn how to be a peacemaker. Peacemakers are very special people. They care about themselves, each other and our environment.

It's not easy being a peacemaker in a world filled with many problems. Sometimes I'm a Scaredy-Cat. I'm afraid to speak out and tell the truth. Sometimes I'm a Copy-Cat. It's easier to follow my friends and do things that I know are wrong.

Being a peacemaker takes a lot of courage. It takes courage to do the right thing. Sometimes I forget but I don't give up. I know it's okay to make mistakes. I learn from them and try to do better the next time.

Being a peacemaker means learning how to get along with all kinds of people. I had to learn how to fight fair. It isn't easy getting rid of bad habits, like calling people names or hitting them. But I keep at it and it gets easier.

Are you ready to become an I-Care-Kid? Do you have the courage? Are you ready to help build a peaceful world? Let's get started. We have a big job to do!

Sincerely,

I- Care-Cat

HELLO BINGO

FIND SOMEONE WHO:

IS A GOOD SWIMMER	WAS BORN IN ANOTHER COUNTRY	CAN SAY "HELLO" IN ANOTHER LANGUAGE	CAN PLAY A MUSICAL INSTRUMENT	HAS A HOBBY
LIKES TO READ	LIKES PIZZA	IS A GOOD ARTIST	HAS A PET	LIKES TO DO SCIENCE EXPERIMENTS
KNOWS A POEM BY HEART	IS LEFT-HANDED	PUT YOUR NAME HERE	IS NEW TO YOUR CLASS	GAVE A PARENT A KISS THIS MORNING
HAS MORE THAN 3 BROTHERS OR SISTERS	WAS BORN IN THE SAME MONTH AS YOU	LIKES SCHOOL	HAS A GRAND-PARENT LIVING WITH THEM	IS A GOOD LISTENER
LIKES TO WATCH BIRDS	LIKES THE SAME SPORT AS YOU DO	CAN RIDE A BIKE	HELPED SOMEONE TODAY	LIKES TO DO MATH

MEET ME

My name is ______________________

And sometimes I am called ______________________

Some words that tell about me are ______________________

My thumb print

____

With my friends I like to ______________________

____

With my family I like to ______________________

____

Something I do very well is ______________________

____

One thing I would like to learn more about is ______________________

____

I would like to become a peacemaker because ______________________

____

As a peacemaker I learned ______________________

I Feel Just Right

1

I have feelings and you do too.
I'd like to share a few with you.
Sometimes I'm happy and sometimes sad.
Sometimes I'm scared and sometimes mad.
The most important feeling you see,
Is that I'm proud of being me.

2

Chorus:
I feel just right in the skin I wear.
There's no one like me anywhere.
I feel just right in the skin I wear.
There's no one like me anywhere.

3

No one sees the things I see.
Behind my eyes is only me.
And no one knows
where my feelings begin.
There's only me inside my skin.
No one does what I can do.
I'll be me and you'll be you.

4

Chorus:
I feel just right in the skin I wear.
There's no one like me anywhere.
I feel just right in the skin I wear.
There's no one like me anywhere.

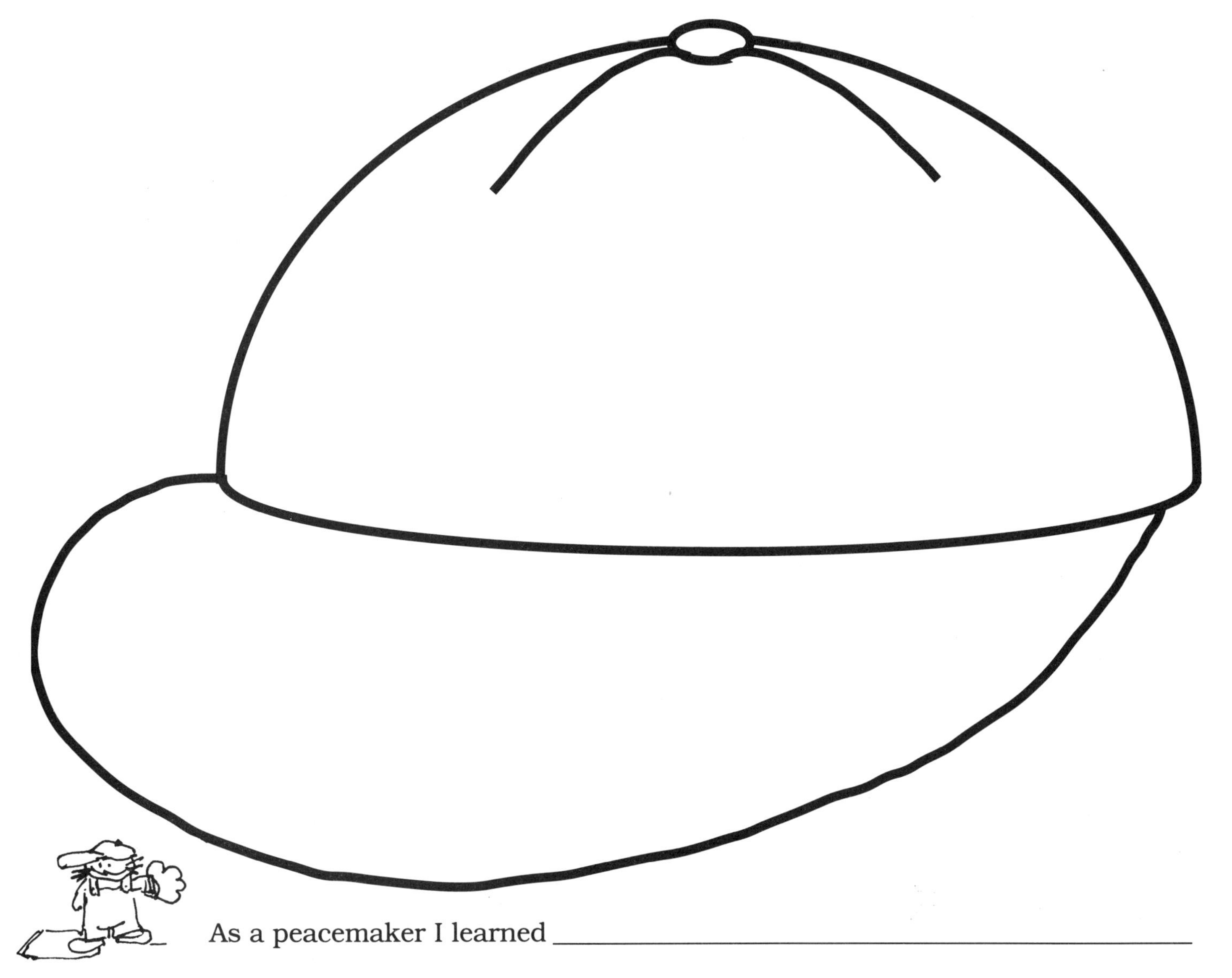

As a peacemaker I learned ________________________________

Hooray For Families!

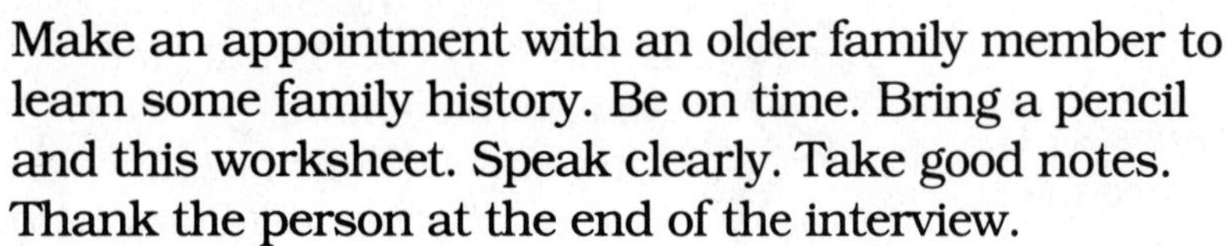

Make an appointment with an older family member to learn some family history. Be on time. Bring a pencil and this worksheet. Speak clearly. Take good notes. Thank the person at the end of the interview.

From what country(ies) did our family come? ______________________________

____

How was life different when you were my age?______________________________

____

What were some games that you used to play? ______________________________

____

What special foods did you enjoy? ______________________________

____

What were some of your customs? ______________________________

____

What values were important when you were my age? ______________________________

____

What special holidays did you celebrate?______________________________

____

Is there anything else that you would like to tell about? ______________________________

____

As a peacemaker I learned ______________________________

THE LION AND THE MOUSE

Narrator: As Lion lay sleeping a tiny mouse ran across his paw. Lion roared and caught the little mouse.

Mouse (shaking all over): Please do not hurt me. I did not mean to disturb you. I promise I will do something for you some day.

Lion (laughing): What can a tiny mouse like you do for a big, strong lion like me? You're lucky I'm not hungry. Get out of here before I change my mind.

Mouse: Thank you, I will keep my promise.

Narrator: Weeks later Lion was caught in a hunter's net. He roared and roared as he threw himself against the ropes of the net. Far away, the tiny mouse heard the roar and he hurried to the place where Lion was trapped.

Mouse: Oh dear! Lion is caught in the hunter's net. What can a tiny mouse like me do to help my friend?

Lion: Not you again! What can a little pest like you do to help the king of the jungle?

Narrator: Mouse thought and thought about the problem. Suddenly, he had an idea!

Mouse: I promised you that someday I would do something for you. I will nibble on the ropes with my sharp teeth and set you free.

Narrator: All day and all night Mouse nibbled on the net. He did not give up. Then, all at once the net burst open.

Lion: Thank you dear friend. Forgive me for thinking that I was better than you. I was so busy laughing at your weakness that I did not see your strengths. You are just as important as I am. Let's be friends.

Narrator: The lion and mouse lived happily ever after.

As a peacemaker I learned ____________________

Sometimes I Feel

Getting a pet

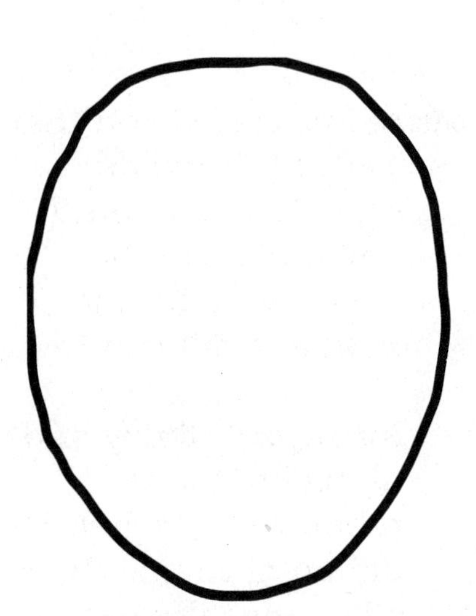

Someone gets in front
of me in line

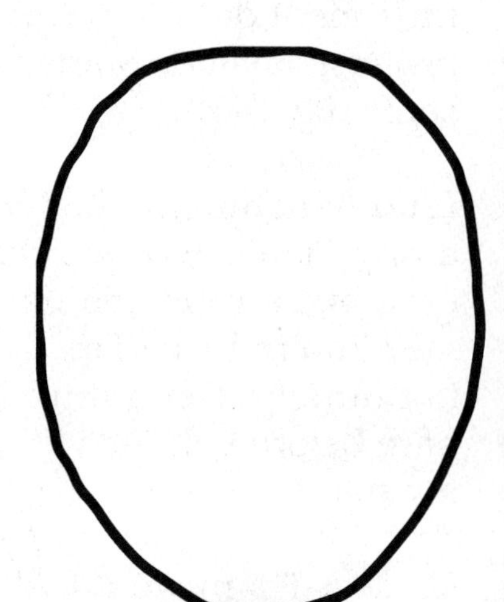

Watching a
scary movie

Sometimes I like to sit alone
inside my quiet home.
No friends to hang around
to make even a tiny sound.

Sometimes I like to share
but other times I just don't care.
Sometimes I feel like loving
but other times I feel like shoving.

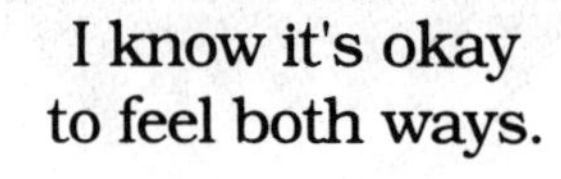

I know it's okay
to feel both ways.

Classmate breaks
my favorite game

Classmate laughs when I say
the wrong answer

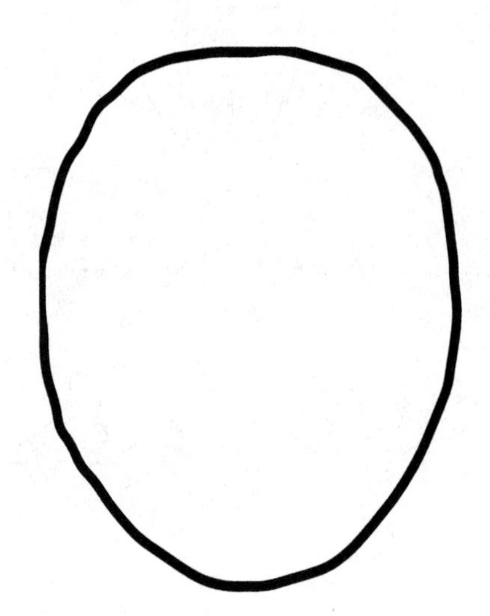

The last day of school

As a peacemaker I learned ____________________________

The First Day

Part One

It was the first day of the new school year. The halls were noisy as boys and girls called out to their friends while rushing to find their classrooms.

Elizabeth stood silently outside the office door. She, Mom, and baby Joey had just moved into this neighborhood. Everything looked so strange! There was an empty feeling in her stomach. Elizabeth blinked away a tear as she watched three girls talking excitedly together.

She wished she were back at her old school. This very minute Sarah and Jennifer were probably walking into Miss Johnson's third grade room. Elizabeth had been in the same class with them every year since kindergarten. They had made plans all summer to be together in Miss Johnson's class.

Then Mom had broken the news.

They were moving to Florida! They would stay with Grandma for a few months and Grandma would watch Joey while Mom started a new job. Then they would find an apartment and Elizabeth would have her very own room. No more sharing a room with Joey! Mom had been so excited as she told the news.

Elizabeth had run outside without saying a word. She was afraid she was going to cry. Her cat Kiki was sitting on the front step. Elizabeth scooped Kiki into her arms and hugged her close as she whispered fiercely into Kiki's ear, "I don't want to go to Grandma's! I want to stay right here and be in third grade with Sarah and Jennifer. I won't know anybody in the new school. Maybe nobody will like me. Maybe the teacher will be mean."

Kiki meowed as if she understood, while Elizabeth's tears dropped onto her fur.

List some of Elizabeth's feelings and put a check beside the ones that you have felt.

______________________________ ______________________________

______________________________ ______________________________

______________________________ ______________________________

Part Two

Now they were here. Mom had brought Elizabeth's report card, the one with the C- in spelling, into the school office. The lady behind the desk told them to go to Room 5, where Mrs. Williams would be her teacher. Elizabeth and her mother followed a tall boy who showed them the way.

Elizabeth's heart sank as they stopped in front of Room 5. All of the children were already seated at their desks. Elizabeth felt her face flush as they all turned and stared at her. Mrs. Williams walked toward the door. Elizabeth's stomach fluttered as her mother smiled and said, "Good morning. I'm Mrs. Perry. This is my daughter, Elizabeth. She is a new student. The office told us to come here."

Mrs. Williams smiled, "I'm very glad to meet you. Come in, Elizabeth. We have a seat for you right over here." Elizabeth's mother gave her daughter a hug and turned to leave. Elizabeth suddenly felt very small.

Mrs. Williams took Elizabeth to the third seat in the second row. Then she said to a girl seated next to her, "Gina, this is Elizabeth Perry. Will you be her special friend today? Introduce her to the other children and help her find her way around the school."

Elizabeth stared down at her desk as Gina said, "I sure will, Mrs. Williams."

Mrs. Williams began to explain to the class that they should work very hard this year so that they could take home a good report card to show their parents.

Gina was writing something on a little piece of paper. Then she folded it up into a tiny square. Mrs. Williams didn't seem to notice. When Mrs. Williams turned to write on the chalkboard, Gina quickly dropped the paper on Elizabeth's desk. Elizabeth closed her hand over the paper and put her hand in her lap. Her heart pounded. Should she open it up? What will it say?

What do you think Gina wrote in the note?

Part Three

Elizabeth carefully unfolded the paper and read:

Tony and I will save a place for you at lunch. Try to get next to me when we line up.

Your friend,
Gina

Elizabeth nodded her head and smiled as Gina turned quickly to look in her direction. Suddenly she knew that she was going to like her new school!

Mrs. Williams was saying, "It is very important for you to have a special place at home to keep all of your school materials together."

Elizabeth looked around the room. She wondered which of the children was Tony.

Write a story telling about a first time experience.

The First Time

As a peacemaker I learned ______________________

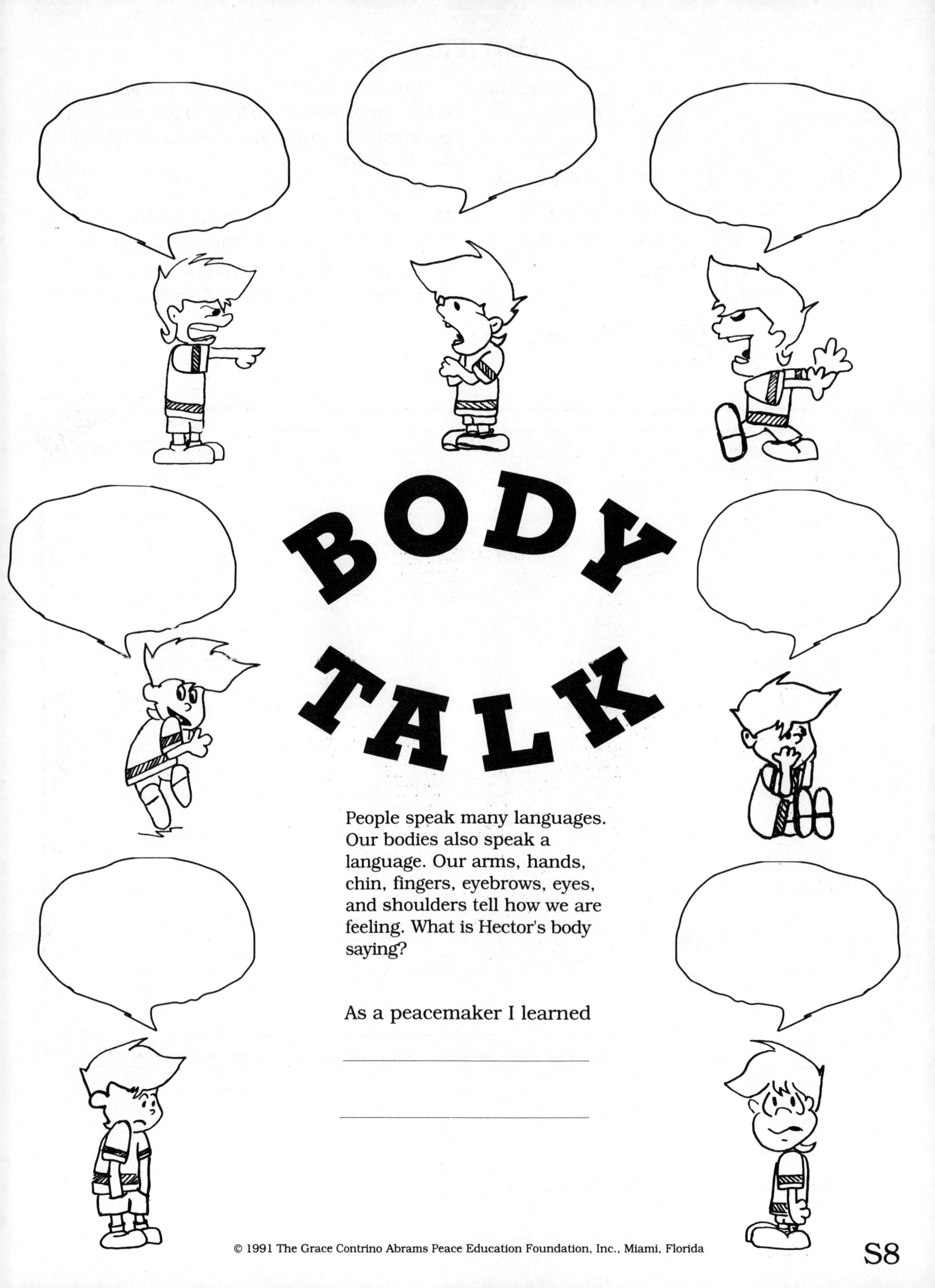

BODY TALK

People speak many languages. Our bodies also speak a language. Our arms, hands, chin, fingers, eyebrows, eyes, and shoulders tell how we are feeling. What is Hector's body saying?

As a peacemaker I learned

____

____

My Temper-a-ture

My Temperature's Rising

My temperature's rising
I'm kinda sad.
Someone pushed me
and made me mad.

My temperature's rising
I'm quite annoyed.
Someone took
my favorite toy.

My temperature's rising
I'm boiling mad.
My friend told a lie
and insulted my dad.

My temperature's rising
I'm about to burst.
He called my momma a name
and I want to curse.

But, I know what to do
When I feel this way.
I know to count to ten
and then to say,

"I feel angry when
you do this to me.
Please stop right now
and friends we will be."

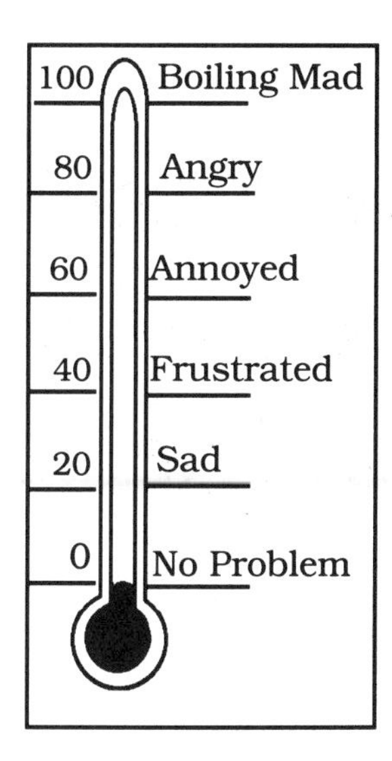

When someone calls me a name, I ______

______

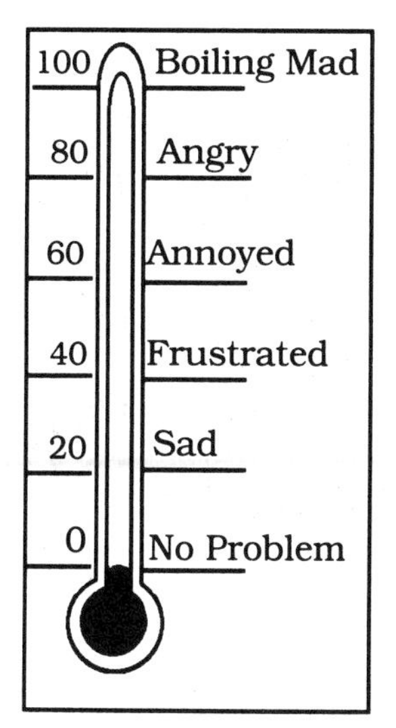

When someone pushes me, I ______

______

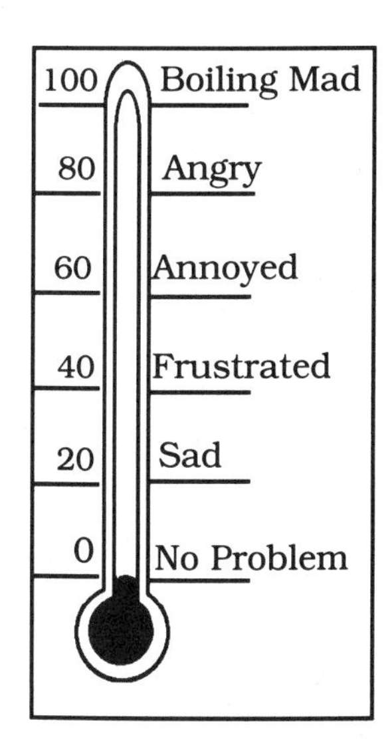

When someone teases me, I ______

______

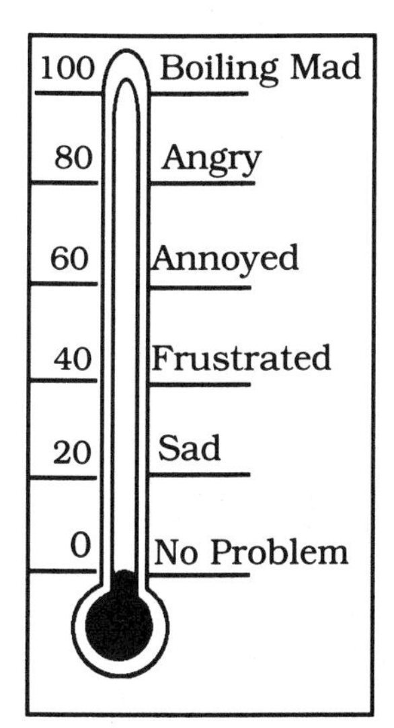

When someone tattles on me, I ______

______

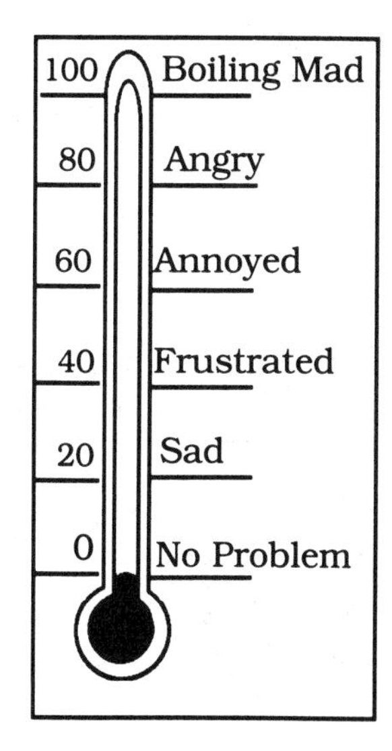

When someone says things about me that are not true, I______

______

As a peacemaker I learned ______

Rules for Fighting Fair

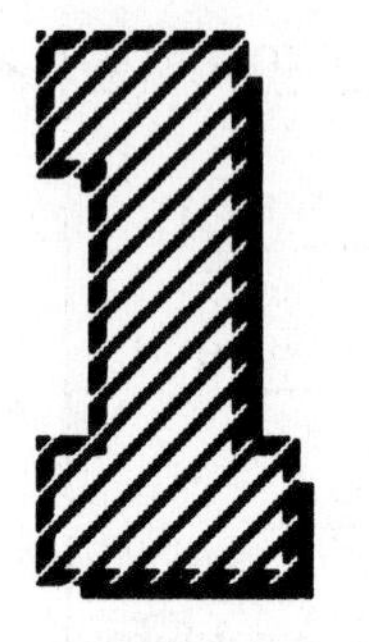

We find out the problem.

We attack the problem, not the person.

We listen to each other.

We care about each other's feelings.

We are responsible for what we say and do.

FOULS

- Blaming
- Getting Even
- Hitting
- Making Excuses
- Name Calling
- Bossing
- Not Listening
- Teasing
- Put-downs
- Threats

What Do You See?

What kept you from seeing the "whole" picture at first? ______________________________

____

When you are in a conflict, what are some things you can do to see the other person's side of the story? ______________________________

____

As a peacemaker I learned ______________________________

What's the Problem?

Look at the pictures below and fill in the balloons with what you think each person is saying.

The problem is ______________________________

The problem is ______________________________

The problem is ______________________________

The problem is ______________________________

A Bundle of Sticks

Narrator: Once upon a time there was a man who had four sons who would always argue and fight. Father loved his sons but he did not like to listen to them fight.

Father: What can I do to show my sons that fighting is not good for them? (He thought and thought for a long time.)

Narrator: One day Father called his sons and showed them a bundle of sticks.

Father: Which of you can break this bundle of sticks?

Fours sons: (yelling together) I can! I can! I can!

Narrator: Son #1 tried but could not break the bundle.

Son #1: I could do it but a mosquito flew into my ear!

Other brothers: (laughing) Baby, Baby!

Narrator: Son #2 tried but could not break the bundle.

Son #2: I could do it but the sun got in my eyes!

Other brothers: (laughing) Baby, Baby!

Narrator: Son #3 tried but could not break the bundle.

Son #3: I could do it but I just didn't feel like it! It's a stupid contest anyway!

Other brothers: (laughing) Baby, Baby!

Narrator: All this time, Son #4 had been quietly watching his brothers trying to break the bundle of sticks. Now he stepped forward.

Son #4: Let me try.

Other brothers: (laughing) Baby, Baby, you couldn't break a toothpick.

Son #4: That may be true. I am not strong like all of you, but I have an idea.

Other brothers: (laughing) How can ideas break bundles of sticks?

Father: Tell us your idea, Son. Ideas have great power.

Son #4 Let us take the bundle apart. Each of us will take a few sticks. Together we can break them.

Narratator: And so they did.

Father: (smiling) My sons, each of you alone is weak like a single stick. But by working together as friends, you are as strong as the bundle of sticks.

As a peacemaker I learned ______________________________

Where Can He Be?

One day an old man and his donkey were walking down the road. They were going to the market in a nearby village. The donkey's back was piled high with baskets that the man was going to sell at the market. With the money he got he was going to buy many things. He was thinking of these things as they walked.

"My friend," the man said to his donkey. "I will buy a new pot for my wife so she can make some delicious soup. I will buy some straw to make more fine baskets to sell. I will buy grain for my chickens and I will buy some sweet hay for you to eat while we are at the market."

As they walked along, the man wiped his face with a large handkerchief, for it was hot and they had walked far that morning. "Let's rest beside these trees," he said.

While they rested some other travelers stopped also. A woman with a small boy sat down under a tree. The boy was saying, "Mother, I will work very hard. I will help you sell all the rugs you have made. Then may I have some money to buy a small cake? A spicy one with nuts in it? Please?"

His mother smiled as she shook her head. "No, my son. There will not be enough money for even a small cake today. I must buy shoes for your sister, some thread for grandmother, and wool to weave more rugs to sell. Here, take some of this bread I baked this morning."

As he sat eating his bread the boy heard someone speaking. The old man and his donkey were starting out on the road again. The man was saying, "It is so hot and I am an old man. If only I had someone to help me unload my baskets at the market! I have a few coins. I could pay someone to help me."

The boy stood up. "I can help you," he called out to the man. "I am strong. I can work hard." The old man stopped. Looking at his mother the boy said, "May I help the man, please, Mother?"

"Yes, my son. After we unpack our rugs you may help the man."

The old man spoke. "Thank you. My donkey and I will wait for you under the oak tree beside the fountain in the town square." And they started down the road.

He was thinking about these things as he and his mother started down the road to the market.

When they arrived the boy and his mother quickly unpacked the beautiful rugs. Then he ran off to find the old man. "Where did he say he would wait for me?" the boy said to himself as he looked along streets crowded with people buying and selling goods. He ran past the baker's stand where he could smell spicy cakes. He looked among the fruit sellers, but he could not find the old man and his donkey.

Meanwhile, the old man and his donkey stood under the oak tree beside the fountain in the town square. "Ah, my friend," the old man said to his donkey. "We must get our baskets ready to sell. Where is the boy who said he would help us?" He placed his baskets carefully on a blanket he had laid on the ground. Then he gave his donkey a drink of water from the fountain.

"Children!" he said to the donkey, "They forget so quickly when there is work to do!"

Write about a time when you didn't listen carefully to someone and it caused a problem for you.

____

____

____

____

____

____

____

____

As a peacemaker I learned ______________________________

Steps to I Care Listening

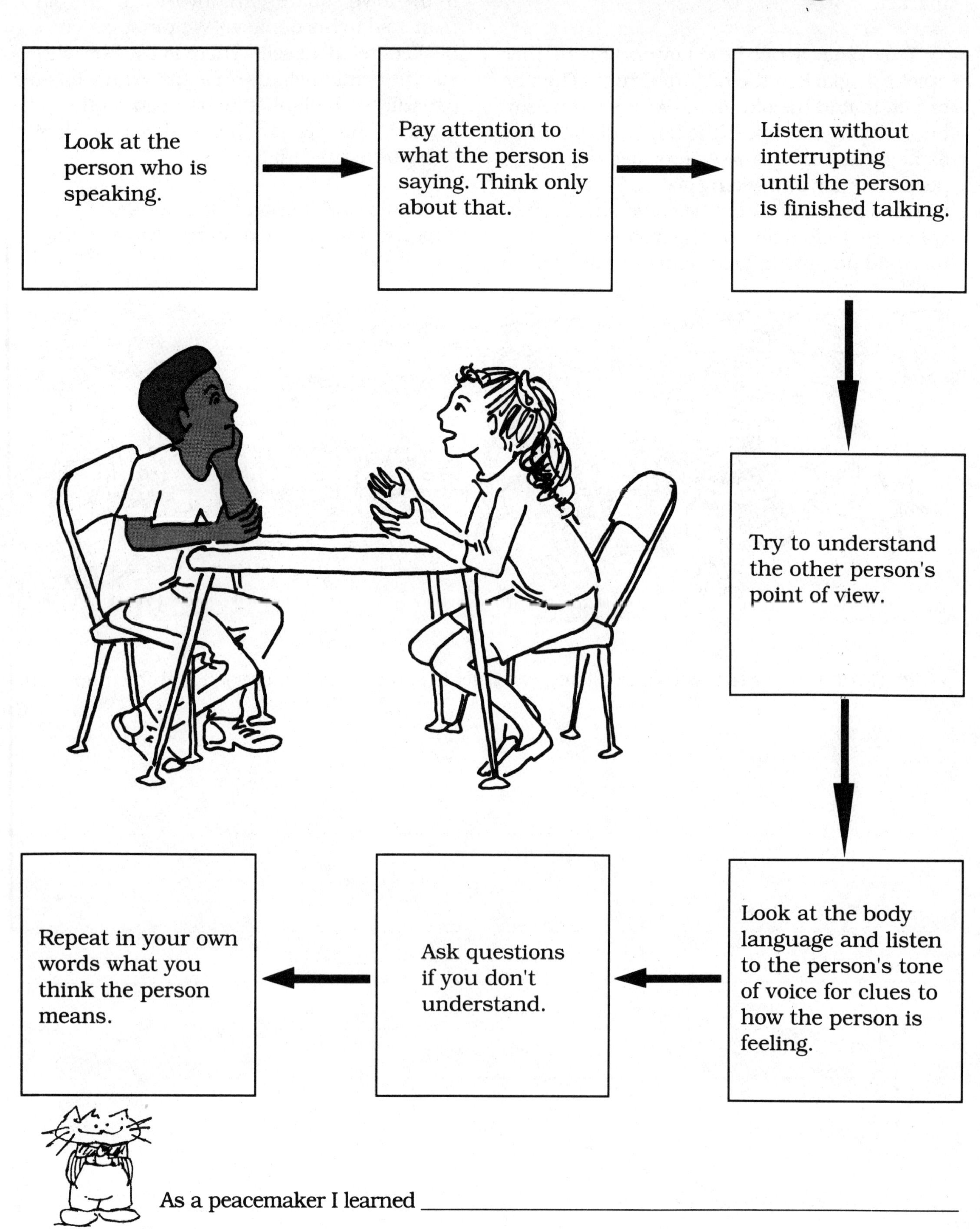

Different Strokes for Different Folks?

When we have a conflict, do we treat people we know and care about differently from people we don't know or like? Let's see!

Version 1

Chandia's class is playing kickball and she is up. After two strikes, she kicks the ball hard. Chandia starts running as fast as she can. Kelly is on the other team. Kelly gets the ball and runs towards the base. Chandia bumps into Kelly and knocks her down. Chandia and Kelly have been in the same class for two years. They are best friends.

Write in the bubble what you think Chandia and Kelly will say to each other.

Version 2

Chandia and Kelly don't really know each other. Chandia moved into the neighborhood last month. She pretends to be tough because it is scary going to a new school. Kelly thinks Chandia is "stuck up" because she doesn't smile. Chandia feels bad because Kelly hasn't talked to her.

Write in the bubble what you think Chandia and Kelly will say to each other.

Remember, even someone you don't like:

- ♥ has feelings just like you but might be afraid to show them
- ♥ wants to solve the problem but might not know how to begin
- ♥ wants to trust you and be trusted by you
- ♥ will work with you if there is a feeling of respect and trust

As a peacemaker I learned ______________________________

Am I a Puppet?

It's Not My Fault!

I'm a puppet on a string
You made me do that terrible thing.
You pulled my string
And made my arm fling.
And now I broke the pretty bird's wing.

But I didn't do it!
You did it to me.
It's not my fault
Don't you agree?

He Made Me Do It!

Josh and Rick were fooling around in the school bathroom. Josh wanted Rick to be his friend because he thought that Rick was real "cool."

"Let's not hurry back to class," said Rick."I hate spelling."

"Me too!" agreed Josh.

"Let's wet some paper towels and throw them at the ceiling," said Rick.

"Good idea," replied Josh.

The boys were having so much fun that they didn't hear Mr. Jones, the custodian, come in. His booming voice stopped the boys in their tracks.

"Okay, come with me! You can explain this to the principal," he yelled.

"Josh, tell me what happened," said the principal.

"Rick made me do it," Josh said. "It's not my fault."

Is it ? ? ?

Tell about a time a friend or a classmate tried to "make" you do something you didn't want to do.

____

____

____

____

____

How are you like the puppet in the poem?

____

____

____

How are you different?

____

____

____

As a peacemaker I learned______________________________

The Boy Who Cried Wolf

Narrator: Once upon a time there lived a shepherd boy who took care of his father's sheep. Every day he took the sheep to eat grass in the meadow, which was at the foot of the mountain near a dark forest. His father told him that it was important to watch out for the hungry wolf who might attack the sheep and eat them up.

Father: If you see a wolf, I want you to scream **WOLF** so that the people from the village will come to save the sheep. Do you understand?

Boy: Yes, Father. I will scream **WOLF** if I see a wolf.

Narrator: It was very boring watching the sheep day after day.

Boy: I wonder what will happen if I call **WOLF.** Let me see. **WOLF! WOLF!**

Narrator: The people from the village came running from all directions. They had all kinds of farm tools in their hands to fight the wolf. They were out of breath.

Villagers: (whispering) Where is the wolf?

Boy: I was only kidding. I didn't see a wolf. I only wanted to see if you would come.

Villagers: (angrily) Don't do that again!

Narrator: Away they went, muttering under their breath. A week passed by.

Boy: I want to have some fun. I am bored. (screaming) **WOLF! WOLF! WOLF!**

Narrator: Again, the people from the village came running from all directions with their farm tools. They were out of breath.

Villagers: whispering) Where is the wolf?

Boy: (laughing) I was only kidding. I didn't see a wolf. I wanted to see some action.

Villagers: (angrily) We are warning you. Don't do that again!

Narrator: Away they went, muttering under their breath. Another week went by. It was late afternoon and the shepherd boy was ready to bring the sheep back to the village. All of a sudden, he spotted a wolf..

Boy: (frightened) **WOLF! WOLF! WOLF! Hurry, hurry!**

Narrator: The wolf started attacking the sheep.

Boy: (louder and louder) **WOLF! WOLF! WOLF!**

Villagers: (laughing) It's only that silly boy. Don't listen to him.

Narrator: No one came. The wolf ate many sheep. The shepherd boy returned to the village with the rest of the sheep. He felt very sad.

Father: Son, where are all the sheep?

Boy: Father, I called **WOLF** over and over again. Why didn't anyone come?

Father: Son, no one believed you.

As a peacemaker I learned ______________________________

FIGHTING FAIR FLAIR

BOYS: Did you ever have a problem
that made you sad?
Did you ever have a fight
that made you feel bad?

GIRLS: Listen to this.
It was made for you.
To help settle fights
and problems, too.

ALL: Use the fighting fair flair.
Show that you care!

BOYS: Got a problem?
Well, don't despair!
We know a way
to fight fair.

GIRLS: I care for you.
You care for me.
'Cause we are one
big family.

ALL: Use the fighting fair flair.
Show that you care!

SOLO 1: Find out the problem
and you will see,
That we can solve it,
you and me.

SOLO 2 : If we keep
love in our hearts,
Fear won't come
to tear us apart.

ALL: Use the fighting fair flair.
Show that you care!

SOLO 3: Attack the problem,
not the person.
If you don't do this
the problem will worsen.

SOLO 4: Listen carefully
without placing blame.
Do not boss
or call people names.

SOLO 5: Do not threaten,
that's not the way.
Talk with respect,
watch what you say.

SOLO 6: Care about
each other's feelings.
Think about them
in all your dealings.

ALL: Use the fighting fair flair.
Show that you care!

BOYS: We're responsible for
what we say and do.
We don't make excuses,
we say what's true!

GIRLS: We never get even
or threaten or hurt.
We use love instead,
'cause we know it works.

ALL: Use the fighting fair flair.
Show that you care!

BOYS: So when you have a problem
and don't know what to do,

GIRLS: Remember the fighting fair flair.
It's here just for you.

ALL: Use the fighting fair flair.
Show that you care!

(Repeat three times a little softer each time until it is a whisper)

THE LUNCH BOX

Elizabeth eagerly turned the page. She could hardly wait to find out if Wilbur escaped from the barnyard. She didn't notice Juan coming into the classroom. Then she heard the clank of her new red lunch box as Juan kicked it under her desk.

"Pick it up!" Elizabeth demanded.

"Pick it up yourself," growled Juan. The red lunch box lay on its side. The children in the class looked up to see what was going on.

"Put it back, Stupid, or I'm telling," hissed Elizabeth.

"You tell and I'll get you later," Juan threatened.

Elizabeth reached over to Juan's desk and knocked his bookbag to the floor. "Now we're even," she whispered.

Suddenly Mrs. Williams appeared. "What's wrong?" she asked.

Juan stood silently with his fists clenched.

"He kicked my new lunch box," answered Elizabeth angrily.

"Her lunch box was in the way," Juan muttered.

"He could have told me to move it," replied Elizabeth, tossing her head back.

"She didn't have to knock my bookbag over. She thinks she's perfect," Juan said.

Elizabeth felt her blood rushing into her cheeks." I didn't know what else to do."

Juan spoke softly, "I didn't know what to do either." His eyes were stinging as he fought back tears.

Mrs. Williams nodded, "Sometimes, it's hard to know what to say or how to begin. I think that you both want to get out of this conflict."

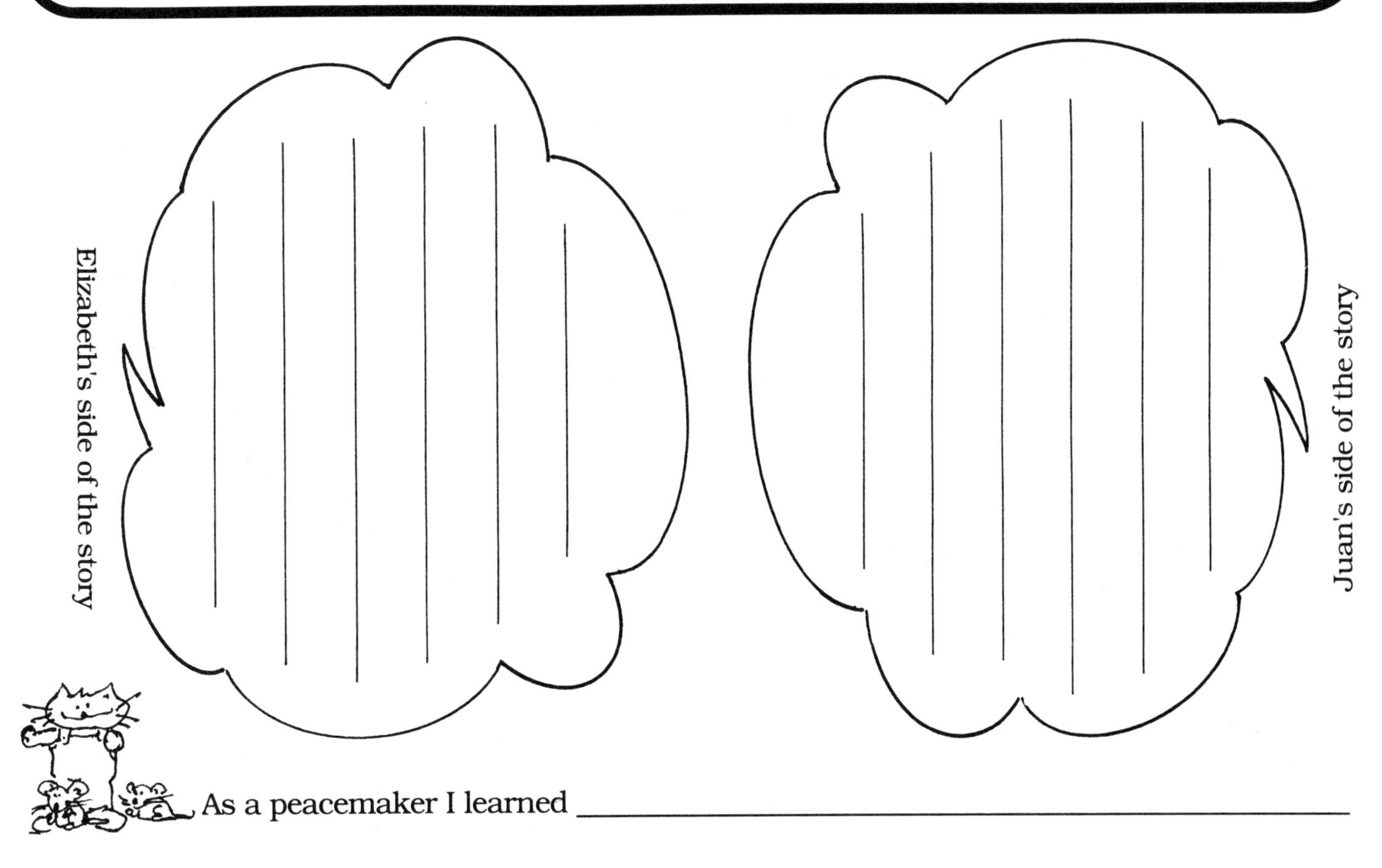

As a peacemaker I learned ______________________________

What's My Strategy?

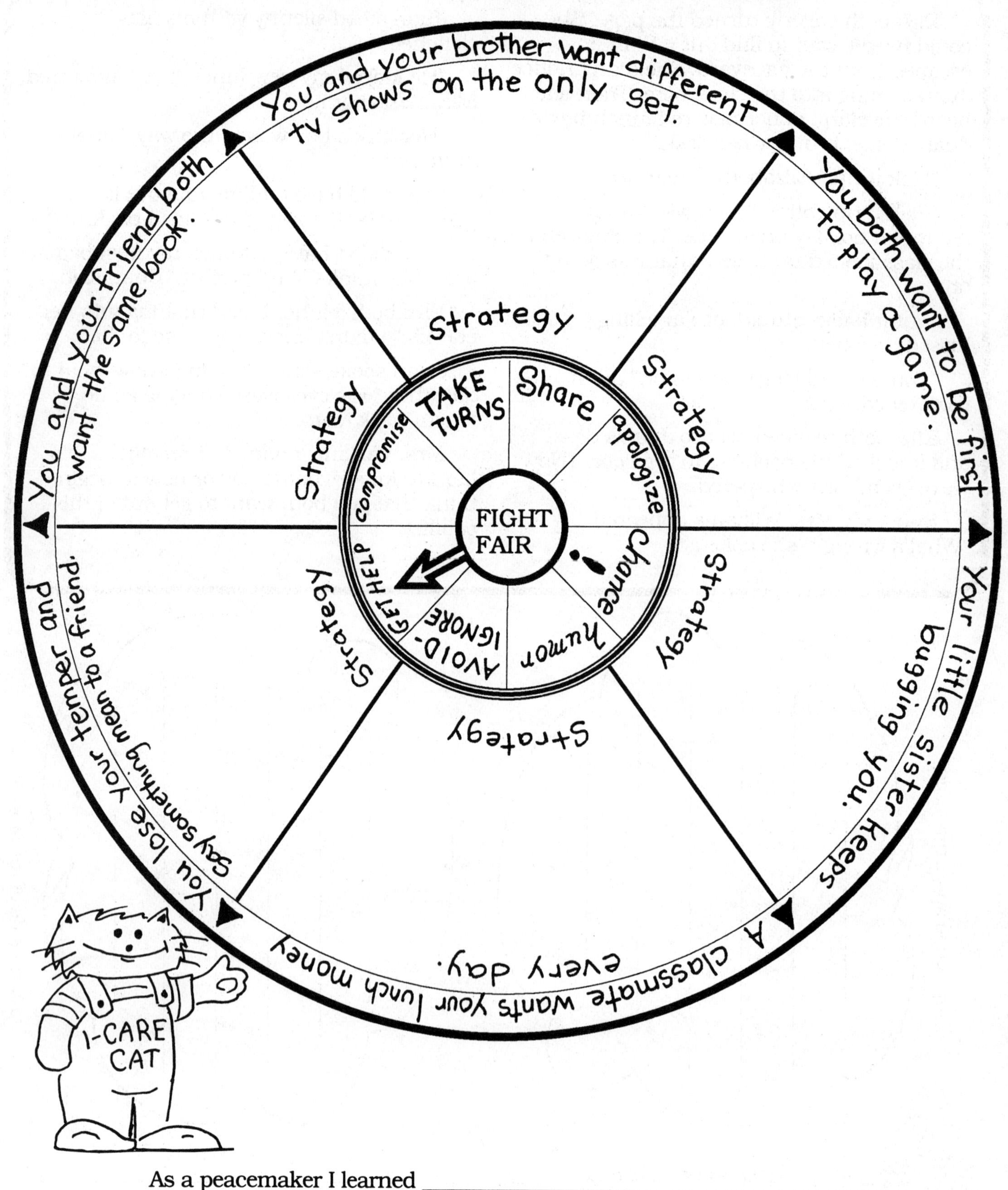

As a peacemaker I learned ____________________

I Can Speak Up!

Sometimes we want to speak up for our rights, but we don't know what to say or do. When we are angry or hurt, we want to get even. Here is a way to help you communicate fairly. It is called **"I Care"** language:

1. **Say the person's name** ...... Steven,
2. **Tell how you feel** .... I feel angry
3. **Tell why** .... when you take my pencil without permission.
4. **Tell what you want** .... Please ask me first.

Remember to:

- Watch your body language. Be sure it is not threatening.
- Stand straight with your hands at your side.
- Don't threaten the other person's space by getting too close.
- Look at the person you are talking to. Speak with a clear, polite voice.
- If possible, discuss your problem privately.

Practice, Practice, Practice.
Remember, practice makes perfect.

Situation 1	**Situation 2**
Joseph knocks your books out of your hands.	You are picked for Sue's kickball team.
Joseph: Just kidding. Can't you take a joke?	**Sue:** Oh no! We don't want you on our team!
You: Joseph, I feel____________________	**You:** Sue, I feel____________________
when you____________________	when you____________________
Please____________________	Please____________________

Situation 3

Carlos wants you to play "Jump in front of a car."

Carlos: You're a Baby. You're just Chicken!

You: Carlos, I feel ______________

when you ______________

Please ______________

Situation 4

Kavita pushes you in the cafeteria line.

Kavita: Get out of the way!

You: Kavita, I feel ______________

when you ______________

Please ______________

Situation 5

You fail your math test and start to cry. Ashanti hears you.

Ashanti: Cry baby!

You: Ashanti, I feel ______________

when you ______________

Please ______________

Situation 6

You miss the ball. Tamara is on your team.

Tamara: Hey, Stupid. Can't you catch anything?

You: Tamara, I feel ______________

when you ______________

Please ______________

Situation 7

Myong Lei wants your homework answers.

Myong Lei: If you don't give them, I'll get you later!

You: Myong Lei, I feel ______________

when you ______________

Please ______________

Situation 8

Frank calls your mother a name.

Frank: Your mama ______________

You: Frank, I feel ______________

when you ______________

Please ______________

As a peacemaker I learned ______________

It Takes Courage

Sometimes your friends do or say things that you think are wrong. You want to say something but you go along with them. Why? Is it because you are afraid that you might lose your friends or be left out of the group?

It takes courage to speak up when you see or hear things that you know are cruel or not fair. Speaking up gives you the power to make changes. People will respect your courage and fairness.

A student wears her new glasses. A classmate says, "Ugly four eyes."

What could you say to the classmate?

____

To the girl? _______________

____

The teacher seats a new student next to your friend. Your friend holds his nose.

What could you say to your friend?

____

To the new person? _______________

____

Your friend throws an eraser across the room. The teacher blames someone else.

What could you say to your friend?

____

To the teacher? _______________

____

Your friend tells a joke to Jan that makes fun of people from her parent's country.

What could you say to your friend?

____

To Jan? _______________

____

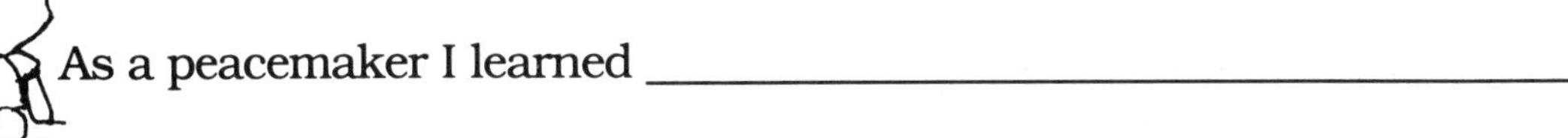

As a peacemaker I learned _______________

What Should I Do?

When you were younger, most of your decisions were made by other people. Now you are older and you have more freedom, responsiblity and choices. You have important decisions to make.

Every decision you make affects you and others, too. Tell what you would do in the following situations. Use these questions to help you make a wise decision.

Situation	Will this hurt me or someone else?	What will happen if I do this?	Will it make me and my family feel proud?	Is this the right thing to do?
1 You are in a video store alone. There's a game that you really want and you don't have any money. "Should I take it?"				
2 The kids at your table want you to join in a food fight. "Should I?"				
3 You can imitate the way a new boy in the class talks. You know it will make all your friends laugh. "Should I?"				
4 Your dad punishes your brother for breaking the TV remote control. You know you did it. "Should I tell the truth?"				

As a peacemaker I learned ______________________________

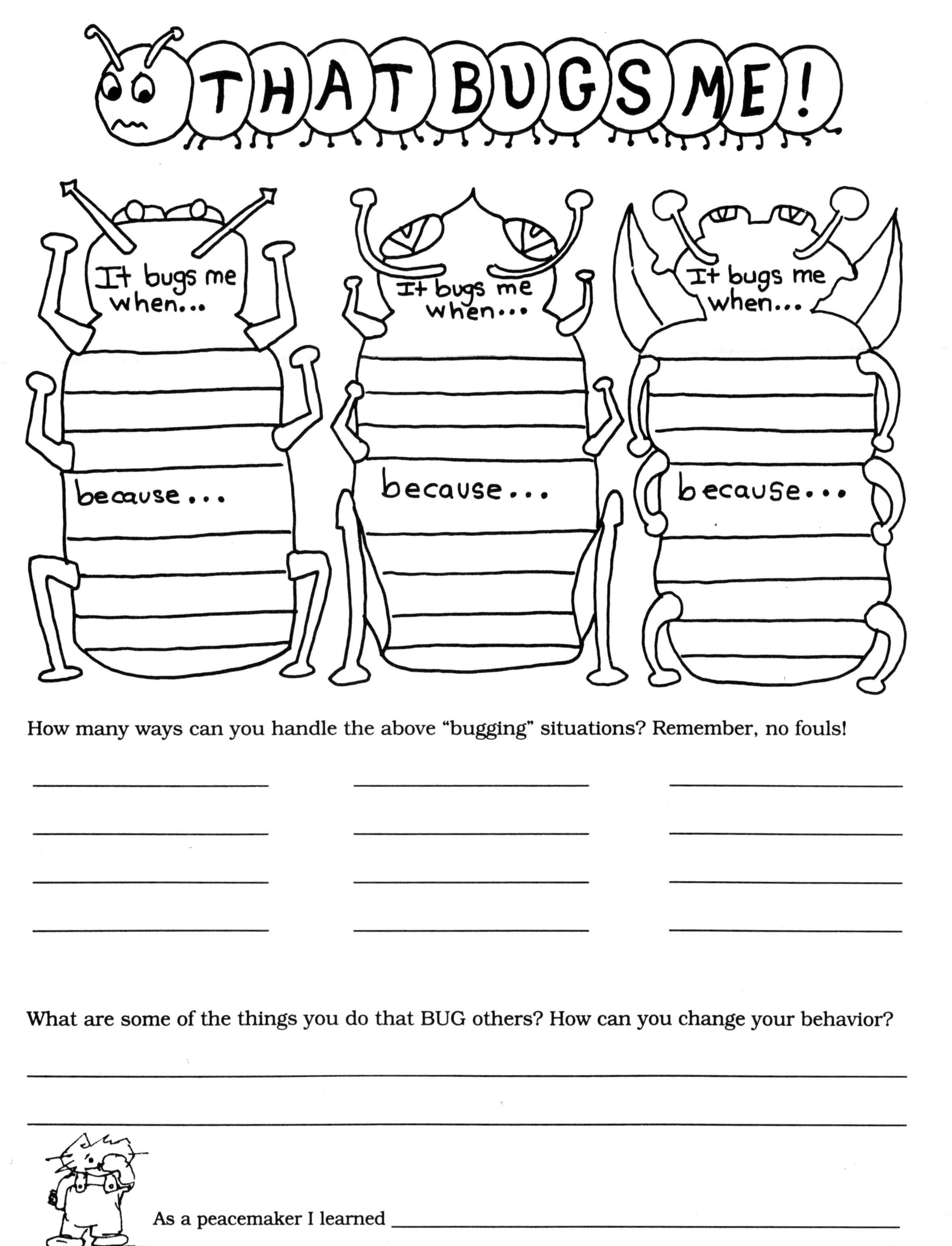

How many ways can you handle the above "bugging" situations? Remember, no fouls!

What are some of the things you do that BUG others? How can you change your behavior?

As a peacemaker I learned ______

Did you ever think that our actions are like links in a chain? Everything we do is linked to other actions. Read the following situation. Then, read the chain story to see how Peter and Jose handle it. Your challenge is to tell the boys what they can say or do to break the chain. Start at Link 1.

Situation: Many students are eagerly taking their clay animals off the shelf to paint. Jose reaches for his giraffe at the same time that Peter reaches for his elephant. Jose's giraffe falls to the ground and breaks.

7
Jose: My brother will get you later!

Link 7 ______________________

6
Peter: Make me! (pushes Jose to the ground)

Link 6 ______________________

5
Jose: No, you can't! (grabs Peter's shirt)

Link 5 ______________________

4
Peter: I'll call you anything I feel like! (grabs Jose's shirt)

Link 4 ______________________

3
Jose: Don't call me Stupid! (moves closer to Peter)

Link 3 ______________________

2
Peter: It was your fault, Stupid!

Link 2 ______________________

1
Jose: Look what you did!

Link 1 ______________________

As a peacemaker I learned ______________________

Belling the Cat

Everyone: The Cat is coming! The Cat is coming! Hide!

Narrator: The mice were afraid of the Cat. They called a meeting to decide what action they could take to outsmart their common enemy, the Cat.

Mouse #1: We have to do something. The Cat always sneaks up on us. We need to find a way to hear the Cat when he is coming.

Mouse #2: I have a good idea. Let's put a small bell on a ribbon and put it around the neck of the Cat.

Everyone: (cheering and clapping) What a great idea! We will all hear the bell when the cat is near.

Mouse #3: That sounds like a great idea, but who will be the one to put the bell on the Cat?

Narrator: The mice looked at one another. They were all afraid to go near the cat.

Everyone: Not I! Not I!

Narrator: Mouse #1 was worried that someone would ask him to put the bell on the Cat, so he started to dare Mouse #2 to do it.

Mouse #1: Don't be such a chicken! What are you afraid of?

Narrator: All the other mice started to chant at Mouse #2.

Everyone: **Do it! Do it! Do it!**

Mouse #2: ________________________________
(Write what you think he'll say.)

What are some dangerous dares? Tell why they are dangerous.

1. ________________________________

2. ________________________________

3. ________________________________

4. ________________________________

As a peacemaker I learned ________________________________

Chicken, Chicken!

Boy Drowns After Taking Dare

Quentin, a 9-year old boy, and his two friends decided to go swimming. The three boys were all bragging that each could swim faster than the others. Two of the boys quickly jumped in and swam across the canal. They told Quentin that it was his turn.

Quentin told them that he couldn't swim. His friends didn't believe him and started teasing him. They called him "chicken."

Quentin didn't know what to do. To save face, he jumped into the canal and tried to swim. Quentin sank to the bottom.

The boys quickly ran for help, but it was too late. The rescue squad could not revive him.

Why do kids take dares that are dangerous?

____

____

____

____

Write in the bubbles what you will say.

1

A friend dares you to steal candy from the corner store.

2

Some boys are daring you to fight one of the kids after school.

As a peacemaker I learned ____

Challenges

There are times we challenge ourselves to do better or to learn a new skill. We take the risk because we know it is the right thing to do!

Svetlana loves to play volleyball. The coach is signing up players for the new season. She tells herself:

If Svetlana takes the risk, what will she gain? ___________________________

If she doesn't take the risk, what will she lose? ___________________________

What's the worst thing that could happen? ___________________________

Manuel's teacher wants him to be in the class play. He tells himself:

If Manuel takes the risk, what will he gain? ___________________________

If he doesn't take the risk, what will he lose? ___________________________

What's the worse thing that could happen? ___________________________

What are some good challenges? ___________________________

As a peacemaker I learned ___________________________

Setting: Mr. Park's fourth grade class.

Narrator: Mr. Parks has just picked three students to help the school librarian carry some boxes to the office. Charles was one of the students chosen. They eagerly left the room.

Luz: Mr. Parks, I don't think you should have picked Charles. He's always doing mean things. This morning, as I was parking my bicycle, he pushed me and took my space. He didn't even say he was sorry.

Class: Yeh, he's a bully!

Sammy: Charles is a great ball player, but he always hogs the ball. Then he calls us names when we drop the ball or strike out.

Anna: Charles picked up my pencil from the floor and wouldn't give it back.

Larry: Charles made me give him a dime to stop bothering me on the way home. Then he warned me not to tell or he would get me.

Jameel: Every time Charles passes my desk he knocks something off.

Gary: Every time we come in from the playground, he's the first one to get a drink of water. He pushes in front of everyone.

Mr. Parks: Hmmm. It looks like we have a problem to solve. I see that many of you are afraid of Charles. We have been learning how to fight fair, how to use I-Care language, and how to listen. What are some things we might try to help Charles stop being a bully? I'll write your ideas on the chalk board. Then we'll practice some of your suggestions.

As a peacemaker I learned ______________________________

The Pied Piper of Hamelin

Once upon a time, the town of Hamelin was full of rats. Rats were everywhere - in the food, in the closets, in the beds, everywhere. The people were very upset. They wanted their mayor to get rid of the rats. The mayor was worried. He put up signs all over town offering 1,000 guilders to anyone who could get rid of the rats.

The next day a stranger came into town. He was tall and thin, with sharp blue eyes, each like a pin. He wore a long coat which was half yellow and half red. He wore a yellow and red scarf around his neck with a pipe (flute) tied to it. He called himself the Pied Piper.

He told the mayor and the citizens that he would get rid of the rats for the 1,000 guilders offered as the reward. The mayor was so desperate that he offered 50,000 guilders. The Piper said, "Thank you, the 1,000 is fine."

The Pied Piper blew his magic flute. The rats came running—great rats, small rats, brown rats, black rats, old rats, young rats. Thousands of rats followed the Piper. He went all through the town and led them to the Weser River. The rats all jumped in and drowned.

The townspeople cheered. The Pied Piper asked for his 1,000 guilders. The Mayor offered him 50 guilders. They argued and argued.

Mediation Role Play

Step 1 Introductions and Rules

Mediator #1: Our names are ______________ and ____________ and we are mediators. We are not here to punish you or tell you what to do. We are here to help you solve your conflict. What are your names? (Write them on the form.) Thank you for coming. Everything you say here is confidential unless it involves drugs weapons, or abuse, then we'll have to stop the mediation.

Mediator #2: There are five rules you must agree to before we begin. They are:

- ✔ Be willing to solve the problem.
- ✔ Tell the truth.
- ✔ Listen without interrupting
- ✔ Be respectful: no name calling or fighting.
- ✔ Take responsibility for doing what you say you will do.

Do you agree to the rules?

Step 2 Telling the Story

Mediator #1: Mr. Pied Piper, tell us what happened.

Pied Piper: I read the sign offering 1,000 guilders to get rid of the rats. I did my job. I got rid of the rats. Now, the Mayor only wants to pay me 50 guilders.

Mediator #1: (repeats) You said that you were offered 1,000 guilders to get rid of the rats. You got rid of them and the Mayor only offered to pay you 50 guilders. How do you feel about that and why.

Pied Piper: I feel cheated, angry, and disappointed because he did not keep his word.

Mediator #1: (repeats) You feel cheated, angry and disappointed because the Mayor did not keep his word.

Mediator #2: Mr. Mayor, tell us what happened.

Mr. Mayor: We were so scared of those rats. As mayor, I offered more money than we really had. We didn't think this Piper could do the job. We have spent almost all the town's money to help the sick people who were bitten by the rats. So, we only have 50 guilders to pay him. He only played his flute for a couple of hours. It's only worth 50 guilders.

Mediator #2: (repeats) You said that because you were so scared of the rats, you pretended that you could pay more money than you really had. Also, you don't think the Piper worked hard enough to earn 1,000 guilders. How do you feel about what happened and why?

Mayor: I feel embarrassed because I don't like to cheat people. I promised money that the town doesn't have.

Mediator #2: (repeats) You feel embarrassed because you don't like to cheat people. You promised money that you don't have.

Step 3 Looking for Solutions

One mediator asks questions; the other writes the ideas on paper. This is not the time for choosing—only thinking.

Mediator #1: You both listened to each other's side of the story. How do you think this conflict can be solved fairly?

Mayor: I'm willing to let the Pied Piper live free in our town for a year.

Pied Piper: I'm willing to wait one week for my 1,000 guilders.

Mayor: Maybe the Pied Piper could have a concert so that he can raise the money.

Pied Piper: I think the town ought to hold a giant yard sale to raise the 1,000 guilders.

Mayor: I could raise the taxes but that would take a long time.

Pied Piper: I think that every family should pay me one guilder.

Mediator #1: Any more ideas?

Pied Piper and Mayor: No.

Step 4 Choosing the Solution

Mediator #1: Let's go over the suggestions you both made and see which ones you both can agree on. Mr. Piper, would you be willing to live in the town free for one year?

Pied Piper: Absolutely not! I have another job in the next town. I'm willing to wait a week for my money.

Mediator #1: Mr. Mayor, the Piper wants to have his money within a week. Which suggestion do you think would work?

Mayor: Really, I like the yard sale idea the best. People have a lot of good stuff. If we sent notices to all the towns nearby, we could get a lot of customers by next Saturday. I think we can make more than 1,000 guilders.

Pied Piper: I like this idea too. I'll take whatever money you make as my payment.

Mediator #2: Is this conflict solved?

Pied Piper and Mayor: Yes.

Mediator #2: I'm going to write your agreement and have you both sign it so there won't be any more problems.

Step 5 In the Future

Mediator #1: What do you think you could do differently to prevent this from happening again?

Pied Piper: I'll get my agreements in writing from now on.

Mayor: I won't promise things I can't do.

Step 6 Closing

Mediator #2: Mr. Pied Piper and Mr. Mayor. Congratulations for solving your conflict. To prevent rumors from spreading please tell everyone that the conflict is solved. Thank you for coming to mediation.

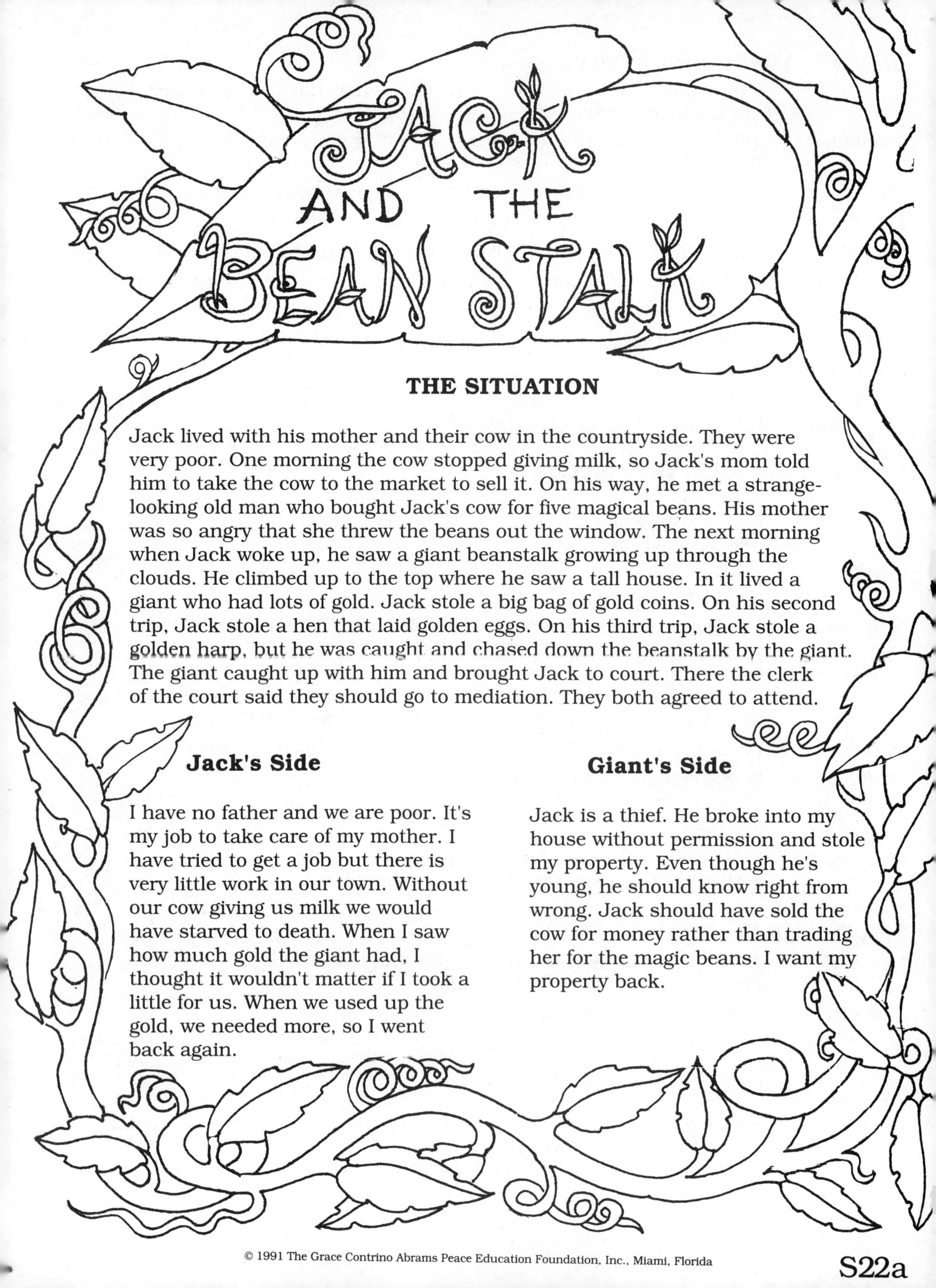

THE SITUATION

Jack lived with his mother and their cow in the countryside. They were very poor. One morning the cow stopped giving milk, so Jack's mom told him to take the cow to the market to sell it. On his way, he met a strange-looking old man who bought Jack's cow for five magical beans. His mother was so angry that she threw the beans out the window. The next morning when Jack woke up, he saw a giant beanstalk growing up through the clouds. He climbed up to the top where he saw a tall house. In it lived a giant who had lots of gold. Jack stole a big bag of gold coins. On his second trip, Jack stole a hen that laid golden eggs. On his third trip, Jack stole a golden harp, but he was caught and chased down the beanstalk by the giant. The giant caught up with him and brought Jack to court. There the clerk of the court said they should go to mediation. They both agreed to attend.

Jack's Side

I have no father and we are poor. It's my job to take care of my mother. I have tried to get a job but there is very little work in our town. Without our cow giving us milk we would have starved to death. When I saw how much gold the giant had, I thought it wouldn't matter if I took a little for us. When we used up the gold, we needed more, so I went back again.

Giant's Side

Jack is a thief. He broke into my house without permission and stole my property. Even though he's young, he should know right from wrong. Jack should have sold the cow for money rather than trading her for the magic beans. I want my property back.

The Case of the Missing Video Game

Place: Classroom

Characters: Zeenat, Robert

Situation: Zeenat and Robert are good friends. They like to share their video games. Zeenat brings a game to school for Robert to take home and play with. Robert puts the game in his backpack. When Robert comes back from lunch, he looks in his bag and sees that the game is gone. He tells Zeenat that someone has taken it.

Zeenat is angry. She tells Robert, "You better find my game or else you better buy me a new one."

Robert yells back, "I didn't even use your stupid game. Why should I pay for it?"

Zeenat pushes Robert and says, "I mean it!"

The teacher asks Robert and Zeenat if they would like to go to mediation to try to solve the problem.

They both agree to go to mediation.

Robert's Side of the Story

Zeenat and I trade games all the time. Sometimes I bring games to school for her. It's not my fault that someone stole the video game, so I don't think I should have to pay. The game could have been stolen from Zeenat's bag. It's the same thing.

Zeenat's Side of the Story

Robert asked to borrow my new video game. It's really cool.

I brought it in and gave it to him. Now he tells me it's gone. Well, it's not my fault. My mother is going to punish me because I'm not supposed to bring the games to school. I want him to give me money to buy a new game.

As a peacemaker I learned ____________________

The Case of the Hurt Feelings

Place: Cafeteria

Characters: Sarah, Toby

Situation: Sarah is a new student at school. Nobody has tried to be her friend. Today she is eating by herself and she hears the other girls talking about the way she looks.

"I don't think she washed her hair this week," Toby whispered.

Toby's friend, Teri, answers, "Yuck! I don't like her."

Sarah hears this. Angrily she takes the ketchup and walks over to Toby and squirts it on top of her head. Toby gets up from her seat and they start to fight.

The girls go to mediation.

Toby's Side of the Story

I was talking to my friends. Why did she have to listen? Squirting ketchup in my hair is disgusting. Yes, we were talking about Sarah but we didn't hurt her. It's not like what she did to me. Is that any way to make a friend? She hasn't tried to play with us out on the field. She just stands by herself. She acts like she thinks she's better than us.

Sarah's Side of the Story

Ever since I came to this stupid school, all these girls and especially Toby, have been really mean to me. I'm just sick of it. Today, Toby said I hadn't washed my hair all week. That's a lie! I wash my hair every night. I can't help if it's oily. Toby really hurt my feelings. I don't have any friends at this school.

As a peacemaker I learned ______________________________

Meet some peacemakers who used their anger to make changes without violence. They helped make a better world. What qualities did these people have? Can anyone become a peacemaker?

Who Am I?

1 I was angry! In England in the1600's, it was not legal to be a Quaker. I was arrested many times when I spoke out for religious freedom. The King owed me money. He gave me land in America instead. I invited Quakers to live in my colony to worship without fear. We then signed a treaty with the local Indians so that our two peoples could live together in respect and freedom.

My name is ______________________

2 In 1888, many people did not know or care how poor people lived. I used my camera to show them the terrible houses and playgrounds. When the people read the story and saw my pictures in the newspaper, they demanded action. As a result, some of the worst houses were torn down and safe playgrounds were built.

My name is ______________________

3 Should people own other people? I was a slave in Maryland. In 1849, I escaped to free territory in the North. I was angry that many of my people were still slaves. I decided to help them escape to freedom by using the Underground Railroad. I helped more than 300 slaves escape. In 1865 slavery was abolished.

My name is ______________________

4 Can you imagine being arrested for trying to vote? That's what happened to me. In 1872, women didn't have the right to vote. I was put on trial. I spent many years working on changing this injustice. Finally, in 1920 the Constitution gave women the right to vote.

My name is ______________________

5 I was the President of the United States. Now, I am working with a group called Habitat. This group believes in people power. Many volunteers help build houses for poor people. What a wonderful way for different people to get to know each other by working together.

My name is ______________________

William Penn	Jimmy Carter	Harriet Tubman	Jacob Riis	Susan B. Anthony

When Clark Kent sees an injustice, he becomes angry and changes to Superman. We can't fly and we don't have x-ray vision, but humans have a very special power. We have brains—the power to think, to make wise choices, and the power to change.

When we get angry or see an injustice, we can use our power to make a difference in our lives and in the lives of others. Kids all around the world are making a difference. They are involved in many projects. What are you doing?

As a peacemaker I learned ______________________________

My Peacemaker's Vocabulary

apologize ______________________________

avoid ______________________________

behavior ______________________________

bug ______________________________

bully ______________________________

chance ______________________________

commitment ______________________________

communicate ______________________________

compromise ______________________________

confidential ______________________________

conflict ______________________________

courage ______________________________

culture ______________________________

custom ______________________________

dare ______________________________

decision ______________________________

emotion ______________________________

escalate ______________________________

fighting fair ______________________________

foul ______________________________

history ____________________

"I-Care" language ____________________

"I-Care" listening ____________________

ignore ____________________

injustice ____________________

mediation ____________________

mediator ____________________

perception ____________________

precious ____________________

qualities ____________________

respect ____________________

responsible ____________________

save face ____________________

strategy ____________________

trust ____________________

unique ____________________

value ____________________

win - win ____________________

Printed on Recycled Paper

ISBN 1-878227-18-1